W9-AXK-554

Cheetah
Speed Demon!

by Natalie Lunis

Consultants:

Craig Saffoe, Biologist
Smithsonian's National Zoological Park
Cheetah Conservation Station/Asia Trail

Cheetah Conservation Fund
www.cheetah.org

BEARPORT
PUBLISHING

NEW YORK, NEW YORK

Credits

Cover, © Andy Rouse/Stone/Getty Images; TOC, © ZSSD/Minden Pictures; 4–5, © Andy Rouse/Stone/Getty Images; 6T, © Bruce Block/iStockphoto; 6B, © Art Wolfe/Stone/Getty Images; 7, © Tom Brakefield/Corbis; 9, © Andy Rouse/Alamy; 10–11, © Gerard Lacz/Peter Arnold, Inc./Alamy; 12, © Gallo Images/SuperStock; 13, © W. Wisniewski/Corbis; 14, © Martin Harvey/Workbook Stock/Getty Images; 15, © DLILLC/Corbis; 16L, © Jochem Wijnands/Picture Contact/Alamy; 16R, © Martin Harvey/Alamy; 17L, © Suzi Eszterhas/Minden Pictures; 17R, © Brian Eichhorn/Shutterstock; 18T, © Graeme Shannon/Shuttterstock; 18C, © age fotostock/SuperStock; 18B, © age fotostock/SuperStock; 19, © Ferrero-Labat/Auscape/Minden Pictures; 20, © Martin Harvey/Alamy; 21, © Suzi Eszterhas/Nature Picture Library; 22, © age fotostock/SuperStock; 22L, © Martin Harvey/Gallo Images/Getty Images; 22R, © Adrio Communications Ltd/Shutterstock; 23TL, © Pal Teravagimov/Shutterstock; 23TC, © Lee Torrens/Shutterstock; 23TR, © Verena Lüdemann/Shutterstock; 23BL, © GGS/Shutterstock; 23BR, © Gallo Images/SuperStock.

Publisher: Kenn Goin
Editorial Director: Adam Siegel
Creative Director: Spencer Brinker
Design: Debrah Kaiser
Photo Researcher: Picture Perfect Professionals, LLC

Library of Congress Cataloging-in-Publication Data

Lunis, Natalie.
  Cheetah : speed demon! / by Natalie Lunis.
    p. cm. — (Blink of an eye : superfast animals)
  Includes bibliographical references and index.
  ISBN-13: 978-1-936087-89-1 (library binding)
  ISBN-10: 1-936087-89-8 (library binding)
  1. Cheetah—Juvenile literature. I. Title.
  QL737.C23L89 2011
  599.75'9—dc22
                              2009053573

For more information, write to Bearport Publishing Company, Inc., 101 Fifth Avenue, Suite 6R, New York, New York 10003. Printed in the United States of America in North Mankato, Minnesota.

062010
042110CGA

10 9 8 7 6 5 4 3 2 1

Contents

A Speedy Cat

The cheetah can run faster than any other animal in the world.

It can race along at a speed of up to 70 miles per hour (113 kph).

That's faster than the speed limit on many big highways.

The world's fastest human can run at a top speed of 23 miles per hour (37 kph). A racehorse can run at a top speed of 45 miles per hour (72 kph). A cheetah can run faster than both.

Human
23 mph / 37 kph

Racehorse
45 mph / 72 kph

Cheetah
70 mph / 113 kph

5

Fast Food

Cheetahs run fast for a reason—to get food.

They hunt and chase gazelles, impalas, and other kinds of **antelopes**.

These deer-like animals are fast runners, too.

gazelles

impalas

Cheetahs also hunt small animals such as rabbits, hares, birds, and lizards.

hare

Creeping Quietly

Most cheetahs live on the grasslands of Africa.

Because of their golden color, they easily hide in the tall grasses that grow there.

When a cheetah spots its **prey**, it creeps quietly toward it.

Then it takes off in a burst of speed.

About 10,000 cheetahs live in the wild. Most of them are found in Africa. About 100 of them live in the Asian country of Iran.

Cheetahs in the Wild

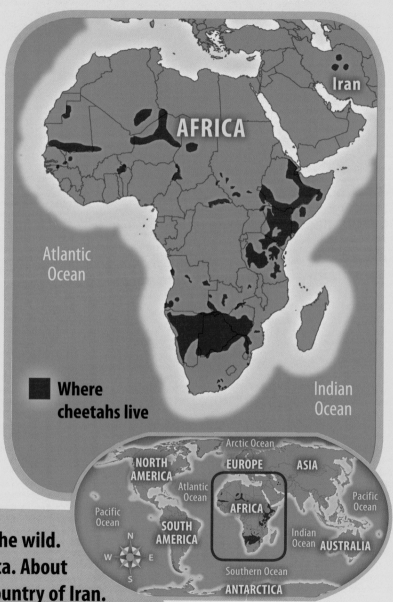

Iran

AFRICA

Atlantic Ocean

Indian Ocean

■ **Where cheetahs live**

Arctic Ocean

NORTH AMERICA
EUROPE
ASIA

Atlantic Ocean

Pacific Ocean

AFRICA

Pacific Ocean

SOUTH AMERICA

Indian Ocean
AUSTRALIA

Southern Ocean

ANTARCTICA

N E W S

A cheetah can go from 0 to 45 miles per hour (0 to 72 kph) in less than three seconds. That's faster than a sports car can pick up speed.

A Quick Chase

A cheetah must catch the animal it is hunting right away.

That's because the big cat is a **sprinter**.

It can run at its top speed for only about half a minute.

Impalas and gazelles, on the other hand, are good long-distance runners.

They can outrun cheetahs in a chase that takes more time.

Zigging and Zagging

When an antelope tries to get away from a cheetah, it uses more than just speed.

It also quickly changes direction to keep the big cat from catching it.

However, cheetahs are good at changing direction, too.

Their long tails help them keep their balance as they zigzag after their prey.

long tail

A cheetah is about four feet (1.2 m) long from the tip of its nose to the rear of its body. Its tail can be almost three feet (.9 m) long.

Ready to Sprint

A cheetah is built to run fast.

Besides its long tail, many parts of its body help it move at high speed.

The cheetah's long legs and back help it take long **strides**.

Its large heart and large lungs work together to get plenty of oxygen into its blood.

The oxygen-rich blood helps power muscles that make the cheetah's body move fast.

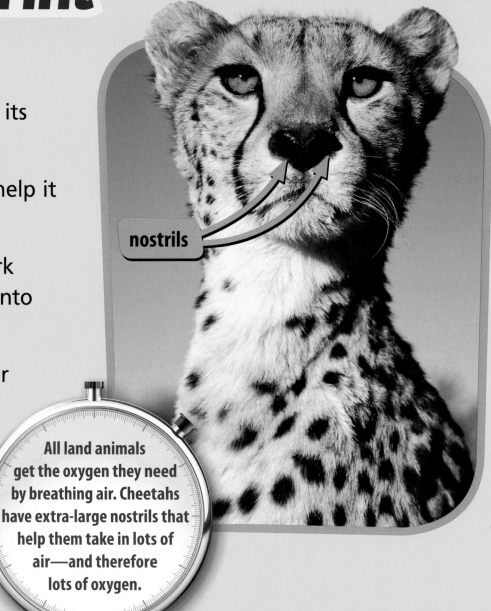

nostrils

All land animals get the oxygen they need by breathing air. Cheetahs have extra-large nostrils that help them take in lots of air—and therefore lots of oxygen.

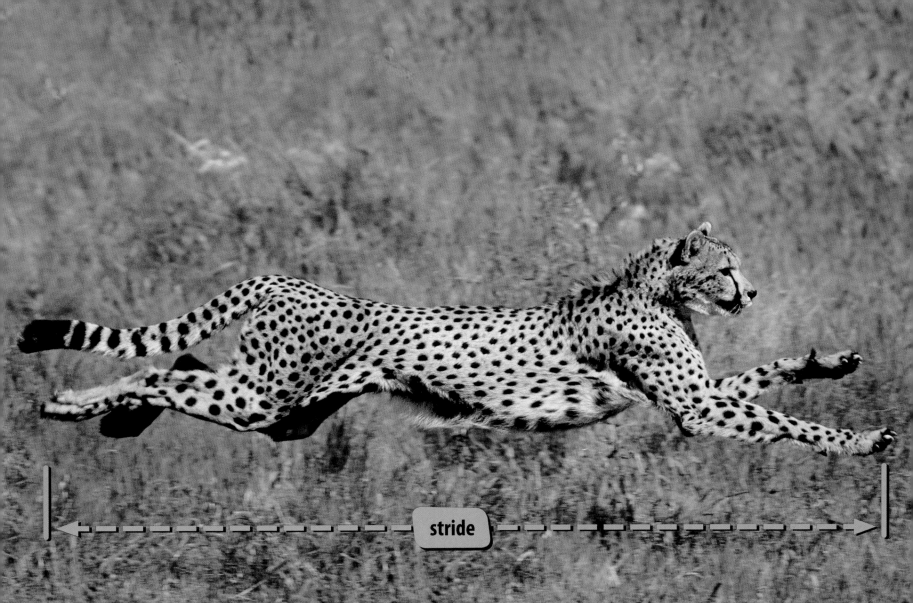

stride

Claws That Grip

Like all kinds of cats, cheetahs have claws.

However, they cannot pull them all the way into their paws the way other cats do.

Instead, a cheetah's claws always stick out.

They help the cheetah grip the ground as it runs—just as the spikes on a soccer player's shoes make it easier for the athlete to grip the ground.

A cheetah's claws are not as sharp as the claws of other big cats. As a result, cheetahs are not nearly as good at climbing trees.

spikes

claws

Dangerous Enemies

Cheetahs are big, powerful cats, but there are animals on the grasslands that are even bigger and more powerful.

Lions, leopards, and hyenas attack and kill young cheetahs, which are called cubs.

These large meat-eaters also steal food from adult cheetahs.

When one of them sees a cheetah eating its prey, it will chase the cheetah away and finish the meal itself.

lion

leopard

hyena

A mother cheetah keeps her cubs safe from enemies by leaving them in a clump of tall grass or another hiding place while she goes off to hunt. Every few days, she moves them to a new hiding place for extra protection.

cubs

An Even Bigger Danger

Lions, leopards, and hyenas are not the only danger that cheetahs face.

Humans have become an even bigger threat to their survival.

Ranchers use land where cheetahs live for farming.

To protect sheep and other **livestock** on their farms, the ranchers often kill cheetahs in the area.

Fortunately, many people are working to save the big, spotted cats so they can keep the top spot among the world's fastest-running animals.

cheetah cubs rescued from ranchers' traps

One way people are helping cheetahs is by setting aside land for wildlife parks. Another is by teaching ranchers how to protect their livestock without killing cheetahs.

21

Built for Speed

What makes a cheetah such a fast runner? Here is how different parts of the big cat's body help it reach its amazing speeds.

large nostrils get lots of air to lungs

long back and long legs help with long strides

long tail helps with balance during fast turns

rounded claws grip the ground

large heart and lungs send plenty of oxygen to muscles

Glossary

antelopes (AN-tuh-lohps)
a group of hoofed animals
that run very fast

livestock (LIVE-*stok*)
animals, such as cows and
sheep, that are raised by
people on farms or ranches

prey (PRAY) an animal that
is hunted for food

sprinter (SPRINT-ur)
a person or animal that
runs very fast over short
distances

strides (STRYEDZ)
the distances covered in
steps taken by animals

23

Index

Read More

Levine, Michelle. *Speedy Cheetahs*. Minneapolis, MN: Lerner (2007).

Nuzzolo, Deborah. *Cheetahs*. Mankato, MN: Capstone (2008).

Theodorou, Rod. *Cheetah*. Chicago: Heinemann (2001).

Learn More Online

To learn more about cheetahs, visit
www.bearportpublishing.com/BlinkofanEye

About the Author

Natalie Lunis has written many science and nature books for children. She lives in the Hudson River Valley, just north of New York City.